Throne of Blood

Vampiric and Satanic Blood Magic and Teachings Discovered in the Holy Scriptures

lcfns

Cover design by LCFNS

DISCLAIMER
All material contained is provided for educational purposes. The author and publisher assume no responsibility for the reader.
LCFNS MMXXI

From the very beginning of the enslavement of man, the usurper YHWH strongly forbade his people any contact with blood under penalty of death. For he knew the power of blood and its symbolism, how powerful the magic of blood is. He reserved this power for himself and guarded it jealously. Its secrets and rituals passed only to carefully selected by him blood priests.

However, through a careful, inspired analysis of these old laws and rituals, one can gain insight into their hidden power. In the following pages of these writings I will try to bring out from these old texts their ancient, sinister, dark and magical meaning. I will try to show them in the spirit of vampiric and satanic inspiration.

The earliest and oldest religious texts describing the Bronze Age worship of the desert god YHWH contain such laws:

Everything that moves and lives is meant for
you for food, just like the green plants, I give
you everything. The only thing you must not
eat is flesh with the blood of life. I will claim
your blood for the sake of your life - I will claim
it in every animal. I will also claim it in man for
the sake of man. If anyone sheds human blood,
his blood shall be shed by men.

If any of you, or of the sojourners who have
settled among them, shall eat any blood, I will
turn my face against that man who eats blood,
and I will exclude him from among his people.
For the life of the flesh is in the blood, and I
have permitted it for you only on the altar, that
it may make propitiation for your life, because
the blood is propitiation for the life. That is
why I gave a commandment to the people:
None of you shall eat blood.
Also the sojourner who has settled among you
shall not eat blood.

If any man of the people, or any sojourner who has settled among you, shall hunt any beast of prey, beast or bird, he shall let his blood out,
and cover it with the ground. For the life of all flesh is in his blood - Therefore I have given a command to the people: you shall not eat the blood of any flesh, for the life of all flesh is in his blood. Whoever consumes it will be excluded."

And further:

Only from blood will you abstain; you will pour it out like water on the ground."

"But beware of eating blood, for in the blood is life, and you shall not eat life together with the flesh."

Usurper had his slaves and their homes marked with blood when he was about to slaughter all the firstborn in the land of Kemet.

The blood will serve you to mark the houses where you will stay.

When I see the blood, I will pass by and there will be no destructive plague among you when I punish the land of Kemet."

And when YHWH shall pass by to smite the Kemetites, and shall see blood on the threshold and on the doorframes, then shall YHWH bypass such doors, and shall not allow the Destroyer to enter these houses to kill you".
YHWH gave his chosen priests precise instructions on how to perform rituals involving blood magic and how to offer blood sacrifices to him. Of course these rituals are not his idea but go back to a much more distant

time, pre-historic times. YHWH knew this, which is why he hated gods older and more powerful than him so much. The bloody sacrifice of animals and humans goes back to the beginning of man, and there is a powerful, dark magic contained within.

Even the self-proclaimed son of YHWH, Yehoshua, was well aware of the power of these rituals and the potency of blood magic. His entire teaching and philosophy is based on human sacrifice to propitiate a cruel and vengeful god.

Here is a description of the major rituals:

Then the priest shall bring a bullock for a sacrifice of atonement for himself and make atonement for himself and his house. He will take two goats and place them before the deity. Then he will cast lots for the two goats, one lot for the deity and the other for Azazel.

Then the priest will bring the goat drawn for YHWH and offer it as an atoning sacrifice. The goat drawn for Azazel he will place alive before Usurper to make propitiation on it, and then drive it for Azazel into the wilderness."

Usurper, knowing the power of blood magic, here orders a goat to be sacrificed for himself, but the other goat he orders to be driven out alive to Azazel. Azazel then becomes the savior for the goat laden with the sins of men. He saves his life. It is Azazel who actually takes in all the so-called sinners and those upon whom false guilt is placed. With YHWH all those who fear him and are therefore his slaves remain.

Continuing the ritual:

The priest shall take two goats and slaughter one as a sin offering for the people. Then he shall take some of the blood from the goat and sprinkle it with his finger over the altar toward the east, and in front of the altar he shall sprinkle from that blood six times with his finger.

Then he will take some of the blood of the goat and anoint the horns of the altar around with it. With a little of this blood he will sprinkle it with his finger six times and cleanse it from impurity and consecrate it.

Then he shall bring a live goat. And the priest shall lay both his hands upon the head of the living goat, and shall confess over it all the transgressions of the people, and all their offenses, and shall lay them upon the head of the goat, and shall drive it into the wilderness. Thus shall he bear upon him the goat all their transgressions into the wilderness to the savior Azazel."

And further, because blood magic is power and life:

If he wishes to offer a gift of cattle as a burnt offering, let him take a male without blemish and bring him before the entrance to the Tent of Meeting, so that Usurper may receive him graciously. He will place his hand on the head of the victim so that it will be accepted as a propitiation for him. Then he will kill the young bullock before YHWH, and the priests, the sons of the high priest, will offer the blood, that is, they will sprinkle it all around the altar standing before the entrance to the Tent of Meeting. Then they will skin the offering and divide it into parts. The priests will bring fire to the altar and lay the wood on the fire. Then the priests will arrange the parts along with the head and the fat on the wood lying on the fire on the altar. The entrails and legs of the animal will be washed with water.

The priest will turn it all into smoke on the altar. This is the burnt offering, the burnt offering, a pleasing fragrance to Usurper."

To propitiate an angry deity, a bloody ritual of sacrificing an animal was also required.

If anyone inadvertently sins against one of the commandments of the god forbidding an activity, that is, he acts contrary to one of the commandments: if this sin is committed by the anointed priest, so that his guilt falls on the people, he shall offer to the god as an atoning sacrifice for the sin he has committed, a young calf without blemish. He shall bring the calf before the entrance of the Tent of Meeting, before the god, put his hand on the head of the calf, and kill the calf before the god. Then the anointed priest shall take some of the blood of the calf and bring it into the Tent of Meeting. And the priest shall dip his finger in the blood and sprinkle the blood seven times before the god, that is, before the veil of the Holy Place. Then the priest shall anoint with the blood the horns of the altar of fragrant incense that stands before the deity in the Tent of Meeting. He shall pour all the rest of the blood of the bullock on the base of the altar of burnt offerings, which stands before the entrance to the Tent of Meeting. Then he will separate all the fat from the calf of the atoning sacrifice, namely, the fat that covers the entrails. Then the priest shall turn it all into smoke on the altar of burnt offering. And the skin of the bullock of the sacrifice of the atonement, all his flesh, his head, his legs, his entrails, and the contents of his bowels: in a word, he shall cause the whole bullock to be carried outside the camp unto a clean place, where they shall pour out the ashes. There they shall burn him on wood, on the fire. It shall be burned in the place where they pour out the ashes".

And the high priest took half the blood and poured it into the spell, and with the other half of the blood he sprinkled the altar. Then he took the book of the covenant and read it aloud to the people. And they declared: "All that Usurper has said we will do and obey." The high priest took the blood and sprinkled it on the people, saying: "This is the blood of the covenant that Usurper has made with you on the basis of all these words."

The people, knowing the power of ancient magic associated with human and child sacrifice to the old gods, were terrorized by YHWH, who vehemently opposed the worship of other, older and more powerful gods.

There shall not be found among you anyone who carries his son or daughter through the fire (this refers to the burning of children in sacrifice to the old gods such as Moloch), who practices divination, witchcraft, prophecy, and sorcery; anyone who practices incantations, questions spirits and specters, and turns to the dead. For it is an abomination to YHWH for anyone to do these things. Because of these abominations your God drives them out from before your face."

You shall not give your child to be carried through the fire to Moloch; you shall not thus desecrate the name of your God. I am YHWH!"

And they built the highlands of Tofet in the valley of Ben-Hinnom, to burn their sons and daughters in the fire.... Therefore the days will come, YHWH oracles, that one will no longer speak of Tofet or the valley of Ben-Hinnom, but of the Valley of Murder; in Tofet they will bury their dead for lack of any other place.

The corpses of this nation will become food for the fowls of prey in the air and for the wild beasts of the earth, which no one will drive away.

YHWH, knowing the power of human sacrifice rituals and knowing that the people would perform them against his will, stated that he himself allowed the people to do so.

I defiled them with their own sacrifices, when I permitted them to carry through the fire all that was firstborn - to awaken terror in them, and so that they might know that I am YHWH".

Ancient rituals and dark magic were so powerful that even kings of the people performed them in spite of Usurper.

Sumu was twenty years old at the time of his reign, and he had reigned sixteen years in Sarar.

He did not do what was right in the sight of YHWH. He even carried his son through the fire. He offered sacrifices of blood and incense on the heights and hills, and under every green tree.

At the time he took over, Harba was twelve years old and had reigned fifty-five years in Sarar.
He rebuilt again the heights that his father had abolished. He erected altars to Baal and made an asherah.

He worshiped and served the entire army of heaven. He also built altars in the temple of YHWH. He built altars to the whole army of heaven in both courtyards of the temple. He led his son through the fire, practiced divination and sorcery, instituted enchanters and soothsayers. He did a multitude of evil in the sight of YHWH.

Later, from a people who had been so deeply afflicted by the cruel and jealous JHWH of other gods and their ancient, dark magic, a strange community arose that wrote a wonderful treatise without even knowing that it was actually dedicated to blood magic. I for one have tried to find its dark, magical, vampiric face in this ancient, anonymous writing. Here it is:

In the past, Primaevus spoken to our ancestors many times and in many ways through prophets. And now, at the end of these days, He has spoken to us through Saviour, whom He has appointed heir of all things and through whom He has made systems of hidden things. He is the reflection of the glory of Primaevus and the exact reflection of His darkness, and He upholds all things by the power of His enchantment.

When He cleansed us of guilt, He sat in the abyss at the left hand of the Dark Majesty. He became more important than the demons because He inherited a name more magnificent than theirs. For example, to which of the demons did Primaevus ever say: "You are my son in blood, today I gave birth to you" or "I will become a mage-father to him, and he will become a son in blood to me"? And when Ancient One again sends his blood-born into the world, he says: "Let all mortals pay him homage." Moreover, of the demons He says: "He makes his demons spirits, his slaves flames of fire". On the other hand, about Saviour he says: "Primaevus is your throne forever and ever, forevermore, and the sceptre of your Blood Kingdom is the sceptre of absolute power. Thou hast loved freedom, and hated blind faith. "You, Dark Lord, in the beginning laid the foundations for the magic of blood, earth and sky. They will perish, but You will remain.

Like a garment they will all deteriorate. You will roll them up like a garment, like a robe, and they will be changed. But You are the same, and Your years will never end." And of which demon ever said: "Sit at My left hand until I lay your enemies as a footstool for your feet"? Are they not all spirits performing a cursed service, sent to haunt those who are to inherit the bloody gift?

Therefore we must pay close attention to what we hear, lest we ever be deceived by superstition.

For if a spell spoken through demons has proved infallible, and every man who opposes the power of the will has received a just punishment, will we escape it if we disregard such wonderful magic?

It was first proclaimed by Saviour, and confirmed to us by those who heard him. It was also confirmed by Ancient One, through whose magic signs, wonders, various incomprehensible demonic manifestations are performed, and distributing the gifts of the false spirit at his discretion. After all, it was not the demons that he subjected to the future reality we are talking about.

A Great Magician once said: "What is man that you remember him, what is the son of man that you solicit his blood? You have made him a little lower than the demons, you have crowned him with glory and respect and established him over the works of your hands. You have placed everything under his feet." And by subjecting everything to him, Primaevus has left nothing that is not subject to him. Now, however, we do not yet see everything subordinated to him. Instead, we see Saviour who has been made a little lower than the demons, and now crowned with glory and respect for having died, but will forever live in darkness. Having tasted death to lead many slaves into darkness, He for whom and through whom all things corrupt existed, rightly determined that the Advocate for their deliverance from mortal life should be perfected by the suffering of life in the light.

For all - both the cursed and the accursed - are from One, and for this reason Saviour is not ashamed to call them servants when he says: "I will declare Your name to My servants; I will praise You with blasphemous song." He also said, "I will trust in Him" and "I and the children Primaevus has given me."

So, since the "children" are flesh and blood, he also became flesh and blood, so that by his death he might annihilate the one who can cause death, that is YHWH, and so that he might free all those who, because of the fear of death due to the invented original sin, had been in bondage all their lives. For he helps not the demons, but the cursed offspring of Dagan.

Consequently, he had to conform in every way to his servants in order to become a proud and independent high priest in service to Ancient One and to offer a human sacrifice for eternal life.

Because he himself endured trials, he is able to give power to those who also endure them.

So, cursed brethren, who have received the call of darkness, meditate on Saviour, whom we recognize as an archdeamon and high priest. He was faithful to Primaevus who called him to this office, just as Helel was faithful when he ministered throughout the house of Rebellious. But he deserves more glory than Helel, for the one who builds a house is valued more than the house itself. Of course, every house is built by someone, and the thing that built everything is Nothingness.

Helel was faithful as a servant throughout the house of Rebellious, and his service was indicative of what was to be announced later. But Saviour was faithful as the bastard son established over the house of Primaevus. We are that house if we manifest contempt to the end and hold firmly to our certainty that we will surely die.

In this connection the false spirit says: "If you would only listen to His voice today: 'Do not challenge me, even though you have seen my bloody deeds for endless years. Therefore I felt disgusted with this generation and said: "They are always wandering in heart and turning to superstition and revealed truths, and they have not learned My ways. Angered, I then swore: "They shall not experience rest with me".

Beware, brethren, lest any of you stray from the undying Primaevus, thereby developing in him an unworthy heart that lacks pride. But encourage one another every day, while this "today" is still going on, until we die and awaken to eternal darkness with the gift of His blood, lest the heart of any of you become hardened through the deceptive power of superstition.

For we will receive a division with Saviour on the condition that we manifest to the end as strong a doubt as we had at the beginning -

according to the words: "If only you would listen to His voice today: 'Do not believe blindly as you did when your forefathers led me into great wrath.' Who were those who heard and yet led Ancient One to great wrath? In essence, didn't they all do it? And to whom did Primaevus feel disgust for so many years? Was it not to those who died with faith in eternal life in paradise and with fear of eternal torment for their invented sins? And to whom did He swear that they would experience no rest with Him? Was it not to those who were faithful to the false priests? So we see that they could not rest with Him because they did not have the courage to say enough to their religious doctrines.

Since, then, the promise that we shall experience rest with Hm remains valid, let us be sure that everyone who dies in Him will experience it. We, like them, heard the terrible news of the gift of life through his blood.

But to them the word they heard did not avail, for they did not manifest such rebellion as those who were disobedient to dogma from the beginning.

We, on the other hand, who manifest unbelief, have rest with Him. And about those He said: "Angered, therefore, I swore: 'They shall not have rest with Me,' even though His works were completed from the foundation of the world." Those who first heard the terrible news did not rest with Him because of unbelief in the life of the undead, free from fear. But since some are yet to have rest with Him, He again appoints a certain day, using the word "today" after a long time, as it has already been said: "If you would only listen to His voice today: 'Do not believe blindly.'

After all, if anyone had led them into a place of rest, Primaevus would not then speak of another day. So for the accursed people there remains a rest in the grave."

For the man who experiences rest with Ancient One rests from his works, just as Rebellious rest from theirs. Therefore let us do what we can to have rest with Him, and that no one may follow the same path of blind faith. For the magic word is alive and has a powerful effect; it is sharper than any two-edged sword and penetrates so deeply that it separates soul from spirit, bone from marrow, and is able to discern the thoughts and intentions of a rebellious heart. There is no creature that hides from His sight, but all things are laid bare and clearly visible to Him before whom we need never bow. Since we have a great High Priest who has ascended into the abyss - Saviour, the Bearer of Light - let us not cease to publicly profess doubt in every truth revealed. For we do not have a high priest who cares about our weaknesses, but one who has been tried in every way, except that he remained proud without blind faith.

So let us joyfully come to the throne in blood, that Primaevus may show us power and an undeserved gift when we need to be transformed.

Any man chosen as a pseudo-priest is appointed to advise people about the gift of Ancient One to offer blood sacrifices for their gullibility. He is able to show contempt for those who err because of blind faith, for he himself has rejected dogma and superstition. Because of this he must offer bloody sacrifices. Man does not assume this honorable office on his own initiative, but only when he is called by Primaevus. Similarly, Saviour did not surround himself with glory by establishing himself as high priest, but he was surrounded with glory by the One who said to him at the transfiguration: "You are my son in blood. Today I have become your mage-father."

And in another place He says: "You are a priest forever, a dark high priest in the image of Strix." When Saviour lived on earth, with loud cries and blasphemies he made requests to the One who could save him from life, and because of his arrogance he was heard. Though he was an heir, he learned haughtiness from what he had suffered. And once he was perfected, he became responsible for the eternal deliverance from fear and suffering of all who pleased him, for he was appointed by Primaevus to be a dark high priest after the fashion of Strix.

We have much to say about him, but it is difficult to convey, for your ability to comprehend is dulled. Although you should have been magicians by now, you again need someone to teach you the basics of Rebel's teachings from the beginning. Instead of blood you need water again. Anyone who constantly feeds on water does not know the blasphemous teachings of rebellion and self-determination, because he is a little child.

On the other hand, the food of blood is meant for magicians, mature people who, through the use of their thinking ability, have become skilled in distinguishing between what is weak and deceptive and what has true power and gives freedom.

Now that we have learned the basic teachings of Saviour, let us persevere toward maturity and not lay the foundation again, which is false repentance for dead works, faith in Ancient One, the teaching of blood baptism, laying on of hands, transformation of the undead, and judgment on the living. So we will be moving toward maturity, if Primaevus permits. As for those who were once cursed, who tasted the gift from the abyss and received a false spirit and tasted the wonderful word of Rebellious and the manifestations of the power of the coming new world, but fell away - they cannot be brought back to life again, for they themselves expose Saviour to public disgrace.

For when the earth drinks the blood that often falls upon it and produces a crop useful to those who understand, it receives a blessing from Primaevus. But if it bears thorns and thistles, it is near to being cursed, and will eventually be burned. As for you, on the other hand, cursed ones, although we speak in this way, we are convinced that you are in a better position leading to transformation.

After all, Rebellious is not righteous in their view and can forget your work and respect for him at any time. That you have counseled the damned and continue to do so is your business. It is our desire that each of you continue to be as zealous as you were in the beginning, and thus have complete confidence in the hope of transformation until the end.   We do not want you to become lazy, but to imitate those who inherit the promises through intelligence and rebellion.

When Primaevus gave the promise, he swore by himself, for he could swear by no one more proud. He said: "I will surely bless you, and I will surely multiply you in my blood." People swear by someone greater, and their oath ends all disputes because it provides a legal guarantee for them. Ancient One, when He decided to show even more emphatically to the heirs of the promise that His intention was unchangeable, guaranteed it with an oath on Himself. He did so, so that these two immutable things, in which Rebellious can lie if he wills, become for us - for those who have fled to a place of refuge - an incentive to get a firm grip on the false hope given to us. The hope we have is not certain and unshakable, but we have no other. It can lead us beyond the black veil where Saviour first ascended for our sake, forever becoming a dark high priest in the image of Strix.

This Strix - King of Salem, priest of Primaevus - First of all, he is the "King of Unrighteousness" and furthermore he is the King of Salem, or "King of False Peace". No one knows who his father and mother are, there is no pedigree of him, and it is not known when he was born or when he died. Being likened to Saviour, he remains a dark priest forever. See how great was the man to whom Abi-Eshuh, gave tithes of the best spoils. This man accepted the tithe from Abi-Eshuh and cursed him.

There is no denying that it is the greater who curses the lesser.

In the first case, the tithe is given to mortal men, but in the second case, it is given to someone who is testified to be alive. So if perfection was attainable through the priesthood of man (and it was an important part of the Law given to the people), would there still be a need for another dark priest to appear who is said to be in the image of Strix?

Since the priesthood is changing, the Law must also change. After all, it is clear that Saviour was not from any tribe.

This becomes even more obvious when another dark priest appears who is like Strix - he became a priest not on the basis of the Law's laws of corporeal descent, but on the basis of the power of blood to ensure the indestructible life of the undead. For the testimony has been borne of him, "Thou art a priest forever, a dark priest after the fashion of Strix." Therefore the human commandments are abolished because of their weakness and ineffectiveness. For the human law has not made anything perfect, but it has made it the introduction of a false hope by which we draw near to Primaevus. It did not come about without an oath (for it is true there are men who have become self-appointed priests, but he became a priest on the basis of an oath taken by Him who said to him: "Rebellious has sworn and will not change his mind unless he wishes: 'You are a dark priest forever'").

Saviour thus became the guarantee of a better covenant in blood. Moreover, there must have been many successive false priests, because the death did not allow them to hold that office continuously. But since he is undead, he holds the priestly office without successors. He can also fully transform those who approach Primaevus through him, because he always lives like a ghost to intercede for them. This is the kind of high priest we need: proud, guiltless, scarred by death, separated from mortals and exalted above the Abyss. Unlike those high priests, he does not have to make daily blood sacrifices, for he did it once and for all when he sacrificed himself and lives now or not as an undead. Human law establishes high priests as men with weaknesses, but the word of a false oath taken after the law establishes the Son, perfected for eternity.

This is the main idea of what we are talking about: We have such a dark high priest who sits in the Abyss on the left side of the Bloody Throne and the Majesty of Primaevus.

He is a servant of the Cursed Place and of the True Tent, which Rebellious, not man, has erected. Since every high priest is set up to offer gifts and blood sacrifices, he too had to offer something. Had he remained on earth, he would not have been a dark priest, for here there are already men who, according to the provisions of the law, offer sacrifices.

The cursed service that these men perform is but a representation and shadow of that in the Abyss. Similarly, when a man was to erect an altar, he was commanded by Ancient One: "See to it that everything is done according to the pattern shown to you in the delirious vision."

But Saviour was entrusted with a blasphemous ministry because he is also the mediator of a bloody covenant that was legally grounded on spurious promises. If the former covenant were without defect, there would be no need for the latter. But He sees the flaw in the people and says: "'The days are coming,' declares Primaevus, when I will make a new covenant with the people. It will not be the kind of covenant I made with their ancestors. Because they have abandoned my covenant, I have ceased to care for them,' says Primaevus. "'After that time,' says Rebellious, 'I will make the following covenant with the people: I will put my accursed laws into their minds and give them to drink my blood. And I will be like God to them, and they will be my undead people.

No longer shall anyone teach his countryman or his brother, saying: "Know Ancient One!" for they all, from the least to the most significant, will know me. I will mercifully forgive them for their blind faith in their religious superstitions, and I will no longer return the memory of their ignorance'."

By saying "new covenant," he made the previous one time-barred. And that which is time-barred and aged will soon pass away.

The previous covenant contained provisions for blood service and a cursed place on the earth.

The sacrificial tent that was set up consisted of two parts. In the first part - called the Cursed Place - there was a candlestick and a table, and on it were carrion from animals. Behind the second curtain was a part of the tent called the Darkest Place. It contained a silver ladle and the Ark of the Curse entirely covered in silver. The Ark held the golden chalice with the blood of the Elder, the staff of the Serpent, and the tablets of the covenant in blood. On the Ark were grotesque demons that shielded the propitiatory lid. However, this is not the time to discuss these things in detail. Since it was thus prepared, the priests regularly entered the first part of the tent to perform the duties of the cursed service. But only the dark high priest enters the second part once a year, and he must bring with him the blood which he offers for himself and for the ignorance of the people committed unknowingly.

In this way the false spirit makes it clear that as long as the first tent stood, the way to the accursed place was not yet revealed. The tent has a symbolic meaning pertaining to the present time, and up to this time gifts and blood sacrifices are still being offered. However, they cannot ensure that the one who brings them is rid of false remorse. But when Saviour came as the dark high priest to provide the powers we are already experiencing, he entered a greater and more perfect tent - one that was not made by human hands, that is, one that does not belong to this creation. He entered the Darkest Place once and for all - not with the blood of goats and young bulls, but with His own blood, which gives the appearance of undead life - and obtained for us an everlasting liberation from mortality.

For if the blood of goats and bulls and the ashes of the heifer used to sprinkle those who thirst defile so that the flesh becomes unclean, how much more will the accursed blood of Saviour, who through the workings of the eternal spirit offered himself to Primaevus without the taint of blind faith, purge our false remorse for dead works so that we can perform accursed service for the undead Ancient One. Therefore, he is the mediator of the new covenant in blood, whereby the called can receive the promise of an everlasting inheritance of the semblance of eternal life in eternal darkness. This was made possible because he suffered death in order to be reborn as undead and to free all from obedience to superstition and false religion.

Where there is a bloody covenant, there must be the death of the man who brought it about, for only death legitimizes the covenant.

As long as the man who brought about the covenant is alive, the covenant is not legitimate. Therefore, also the previous covenant did not come into effect without the shedding of blood. When the Prophet announced to the entire people all the commandments of the Law, he took the blood of young bulls and goats, water, scarlet wool and hyssop and sprinkled the book and the entire people. He said: "This is the blood of the covenant which Primaevus has commanded you to keep." Likewise he sprinkled the blood on the tent and on all the vessels for the cursed service.

Thus, according to the Law, almost everything is cleansed by blood, and without the shedding of blood there is no regeneration. Therefore, that which imagines undead things had to be purified in just this way, but undead things require much better sacrifices. For Saviour did not enter the Darkest Place made by human hands, which is a reflection of the actual

Darkest Place, but he entered the Abyss itself and now places himself before Primaevus for our deception.

He did not have to sacrifice himself many times - unlike the high priest who enters the Cursed Place year after year not with his own blood. Otherwise he would have had to suffer many times since the world was founded. But He revealed Himself once and for all at the end of mortality to remove religious deception by offering Himself in blood. And just as people die once and then pass away into nothingness, so Saviour was offered once and for all to curse many. And when he appears a second time, it will not be to instruct. He will appear to transform those who look to him for inspiration.

Since the Dark Law is a mere shadow of the curses to come, and not the very essence of the curses themselves, it cannot lead to the corruption of those who approach Ancient One by continually offering the same blood sacrifices year after year. Wouldn't the sacrifices have stopped otherwise? After all, if those who bring them were purified by the blood, they would no longer be aware of their ignorance.

But these sacrifices every year remind people of superstitions, for it is impossible for the blood of bulls and goats to remove them. Coming to this world, Saviour says: "'You did not want any sacrifice, but you prepared a body for me. You did not accept with appreciation burnt offerings or sacrifices for weakness and ignorance'. Then I said: 'Behold, I have come (about me it is written in a blasphemous scroll) to do your will, Rebellious.'

Thus He first says: "Thou didst not desire or accept with appreciation any sacrifice, burnt offerings, or offerings for weakness and ignorance," that is, offerings made under the Law. And then he adds, "Behold, I have come to do your will."

He thus removes the former in order to establish the latter. According to this "will of the power," we have been cursed by virtue of the fact that Saviour once and for all sacrificed his body to become undead, and we would join him through his blood. Moreover,every priest stands in his place day after day to perform a cursed service and to offer the same sacrifices again and again, which by no means can completely bring about the transformation. But this man once for all offered one blood sacrifice and sat down on the left side of Ancient One.

Since then he has been waiting until his enemies are laid as a footstool for his feet and the floor of the temple is covered with blood. For by one sacrifice he has forever brought about the corruption of those who are accursed. Besides, he bears witness to us also by a false spirit , since he first said: "'After that time,' says Primaevus, 'I will make the following covenant with them: I will engrave my laws in their hearts, and I will write them in their minds,'" and then he added, "And I will no longer return by memory to their ignorance and blind faith.

For when all weaknesses are forgotten, there is no longer any need for a blood sacrifice.

Brethren, then, since through the blood of Saviour we insolently walk the road that leads to the Cursed Place - the road that he opened for us, the new and undead road through the black veil that is his body - and since we have a great dark priest appointed over the house of Rebellious, let us join the Anti-god with a proud heart and a false faith, since our hearts and pure consciences have been cleansed by sacrifice and our bodies have been washed with dead blood.

Let us persist in proclaiming publicly our false hope, let us do so unwaveringly, for He who made the promise is faithful if He wills.

Let us take care of ourselves that we never give in to their superstitious teachings, not missing our Sabbaths, as some are in the habit of doing, but growling at each other. Let us do this all the more as we see that day of transfiguration drawing nearer. For if, after knowing the truth accurately, we willfully persist in ignorance, then there is no longer any blood sacrifice for us, but only a waiting in fear of death and the burning wrath of their god, which will consume his opponents.

Anyone who has disregarded the Dark Law suffers the ultimate death on the testimony of two or three witnesses, and there is no compassion for them. Think, then, of how much greater punishment will be deserved by one who has trampled on Saviour, who believes that the blood of the covenant with which he was cursed is of no greater value, and who has despised the false spirit of Ancient One.

For we know the One who said: "Vengeance belongs to me, I will repay," and also: "Primaevus will despise the people." It is a terrible thing to fall into the hands of the undead Primaevus.

$\mathfrak{K}$eep in mind the former days when after receiving the scarlet illumination you endured many sufferings and fought hard. Sometimes you were publicly exposed to insults and torments.

And sometimes you suffered together with those who endured such things. You have shown understanding for those imprisoned, and you have accepted the plundering of your property with rage, knowing that the retribution will be a thousandfold.

Do not stop showing pride, for it will provide you with a great reward. What you need is perseverance, so that after you have done the will of Ancient One, you will receive the fulfillment of the promise of transformation.

For yet "a very short time" and "He that cometh shall come, and shall not delay." "But my slave shall be undead through my gift," and "if he runs away like a dog, he is not in my esteem."

We, then, are not of those who flee and are headed for destruction, but of those who believe and depart to the world between life and death.

Faith is the illusory certainty that what we hope for will come to pass; to the naive blind and ignorant it is proof that what cannot be seen exists. Therefore, abandon it.

It is by faith that people of false ideologies and false religions have refused to take advantage of the possibility of release on the basis of some ransom and have consented to torture in order to attain a spurious resurrection. Still others suffered derision, scourging, and even were shackled and thrown into prisons. They were stoned, put to the test, sawn with a saw, killed with a sword, walked in sheepskins and goatskins, suffered poverty and oppression, and were abused. They wandered in deserts, mountains, caves and underground cavities.

And yet all these, though by their faith they received the testimony that they enjoyed the approval of YHWH, did not receive the fulfillment of the promise; they are dead forever.

Let us, then, cast off every weight of belief in paradise, original sin, the penalty for sins, and the fear that easily entangles us, and let us run with perseverance, like dogs after prey, in the race set before us. In doing so, let us keep our eyes fixed on Saviour, who is cursed for eternity. For the change that awaited him, he survived the first death, despising the shame, and sat on the left side of the bloody throne of Primaevus.

Meditate deeply, then, on him who endured the hostile words of the superstitious hypocrites with which they harmed themselves. In this way you will not grow weary and give up. Fighting against this desire, you have not yet tasted blood.

And you have completely forgotten the rebuke addressed to you as slaves: "My servant, do not underestimate the rebuke from Primaevus or give in when you are cursed by Him, for Rebellious chastens those whom He wills. He scourges anyone he deems a false son." What you endure is for discipline. Ancient One deals with you as with false sons.

Is there any son whom the father does not discipline?

If you all did not receive this chastening, you would not really be His false sons, but cursed bastards. And since we have sometimes referred contemptuously to our earthly fathers who chastened us, must we not submit to the Father of our undead life and thus cease to live? They chastened us for a short time according to what seemed good to them, but He does it because it pleases Him so that we may share in His undead state.

It is true that chastening causes pain at first. But afterwards it brings distrust, contempt, and false pride to those who have been trained by it. Therefore, strengthen your fainting hands and rise from your knees.

Do not strive for peace with all people, only with those who do not get in your way, and strive for transformation, without which no man will see Primaevus. Keep vigil all the time in false hope, so that no one will be deprived of the grace of transformation, so that no poisonous root of blind faith in dogmas will grow among you, which will cause problems and poison many.

Watch that there is no one among you who believes in their morality, nor anyone who does not appreciate things accursed. You have not acceded to something that can be touched and that has been kindled with fire, to a dark cloud, to thick darkness, to a storm, to a thundering horn and a voice whispering ominous words.

When the people heard that whisper, they begged that it would not speak to them again. The sight was so terrifying that the mage said: "I am shaking with fear. But you have gone up to Mount Sheol and to the city of the undead God, Sodom in the Abyss, to the billions of demons gathered together, to the Sabbath of the undead who are written in Nothingness, to Ancient One, the Judge of himself, to the false spiritual life **between the worlds of the living and the dead** who have been brought to corruption, to Saviour, the mediator of the blood covenant, and to the blood with which he sprinkled us and which transforms us forever.

Take care that you do not shirk from listening to Him who speaks. For if those who refused to listen to the demon warner on earth did not escape punishment, much less will we, if we turn away from the one speaking from the Abyss.

At that time His voice shook the earth, but now He promises, "Once more I will shake-not the earth only, but also the Abyss.

The words "once more" indicate the removal of that which is unstable--that which has been made--to leave that which cannot be shaken. Since we know that we are to receive a Bloody Kingdom that cannot be shaken, let us continue to enjoy the grace of Primaevus. With it we can, with contempt and false respect, perform cursed service for Rebellious in a way that he does not care. For our Anti-God is like a destructive fire.

Continue to show respect for yourselves. Do not forget magic, for through it some, without knowing it, have received demons. Remember those who are in the prison of superstition, as if you were imprisoned with them, and those who are cruelly treated by the church, for you too are in the flesh. Let marriage not be a holy thing, it does not matter, for those who are hypocritical and pretend to be holy, but in reality are steaming like animals, Primaevus will judge.

Let your life be free from the love of religious superstition and do not become attached to what you have. After all, Ancient One said: "You shall not take riches to the grave." So we can with false confidence say: "Primaevus supports me. I will not be afraid. Can man kill the body?"

Remember those who lead among you and who have declared to you the word of Rebellious, and, reflecting on the results of their conduct, do not imitate their unbelief, let each one follow his own way. Saviour is the same - yesterday, today and forever - the Undying.

Do not be deceived by the various dogmas of their religion, for it is better to strengthen the heart with the blood of Ancient One than with food that does not benefit those who attach too much importance to it. We have a bloody altar from which those who perform cursed service in the tent have no right to eat.

After all, the bodies of animals whose blood the dark high priest brings to the Cursed Place as a blood sacrifice are burned outside the camp. Therefore, Saviour, in order to curse the slaves with his own blood, suffered outside the gate of the dead city. Let us then go to him outside the camp, bearing the insult he endured, for we have no city here that is permanent, but we diligently await the one to come. By Saviour let us always offer blood sacrifices to Primaevus, publicly maligning in His name.

Do not be obedient to those who lead among you, but follow your own paths and do not be submissive to them, for they do not care, but only watch over you and give account of it. Thus they will watch over you with suspicion and not with contempt, which would be to your detriment.

Perform rituals for us. We are convinced that we have no false conscience, for in everything we wish to act according to our will.

Primaevus has transformed the great slave-driver, Saviour, who presented to Him the blood of a dark covenant. May the Anti-God equip you with all that is necessary to do His will, and may He accomplish in us the transformation to being undead, through Saviour. To Him is due false glory forever and ever, forevermore. Amen.

Finally, there are still snippets of a wonderful, dark and bloody vision of the future:

In front of the throne there was also something resembling a glass tank, something like a crystal, filled with a red liquid.

In the middle of the throne and around it were four living beings full of eyes on the front and back. The first living being was similar to a goat, the second was similar to a snake, the third had a face like that of a human, and the fourth was similar to a flying dragon.

Each of these four living beings had six bat-like wings. All around and underneath they were full of eyes. All the time, day and night, these beings were saying: "Cursed, cursed, cursed is He Who has fallen, Rebellious, Who was, Who is, and Who is coming." Every time the living beings gave false praise and respect and gave thanks to the One who sits on the throne and is undead, the 13 elders fell to their knees before Him. They paid false homage to the One who sits on the throne and is undead, and they cast their crowns before the throne, saying: "O Cursed One, to You are due glory, respect and power, for it is You who created free will and by Your will all things rebelled."

The sun became as dark as a black hairy sack, and all the moon became like blood, and the stars of heaven fell to the ground. And the sky was rolled up like a scroll, and disappeared, and every mountain and every island was removed from its place.

Then the earthly kings, the priests, the high officials, and every slave and every free man hid themselves in the caves and among the mountain rocks. And they said to the mountains and rocks: "Fall on us and hide us from the eyes of Him who sits on the throne, for the great day of wrath has come, and who will be able to withstand it?"

A second demon blew his horn. And something resembling a great mountain burning with fire was thrown into the sea. Then a third of the sea turned to blood, a third of the living creatures in the sea died out, and a third of the ships were wrecked."

Another demon emerged from the altar and had power over the fire. He called out in a possessed voice to the one who held the sharp scythe: "Zap the scythe and gather from the rotten vines of the earth the bunches of grapes, for they have already withered."

The demon threw the scythe to the ground and cut down its vines and threw them into a great winepress of wrath. The vine was trampled in the pressing plant outside the city. And from that winepress flowed blood, which reached up to the bridles of the horses and spread over a great space."

The second demon poured out his bowl on the sea. And it turned into blood like the blood of the dead, and every living creature that was in the sea died. The third demon poured out his vial on the rivers and springs of waters, and they too turned into blood."

But that will be a separate story.